FROM PAIN TO PURPOSE

By
Dr. Jacqueline Fair

INTRODUCTION

When it comes to pain, we look at it in a negative sense. How bad it is and how uncomfortable it makes us feel. Sometimes, we even view it as a punishment from God for something we have done, and we begin to think we deserve it. We become mentally overwhelmed, and it causes us to be in a very dark place. Elizabeth Hartney wrote an article on addiction, and she talked about how emotional pain affects your body; she said emotional pain is pain or hurt that originates from non-physical sources. Sometimes, this emotional distress is the result of the actions of others. Other times, it might result from regret, grief, or loss. In other cases, it might be the result of underlying mental health conditions such as depression or anxiety. No matter what the cause, this psychological pain can be very intense and significantly affect many different areas of your life. While it is often dismissed as being less severe than physical pain, emotional pain must be taken seriously. Several common feelings are associated with emotional pain that can have an impact on both your physical and mental health.

Table of Contents

INTRODUCTION i

Chapter One   How it started (growing up in an abusive home) 1

Chapter Two   The beginning of my addiction/parenthood   7

Chapter Three   The beginning of my deliverance 12

Chapter Four   After My Deliverance 17

Chapter Five   Perseverance: WHAT IT TAKES TO CARE FOR A TERMINAL ILL LOVED ONE 20

Chapter One

How it started (growing up in an abusive home)

As a child, I remember growing up in a very dark place. I grew up in a two-parent home. My father's name was Haskell, and my mother's name was Lois. I was the youngest of seven children. My oldest sister, Bernice, died as an infant. So, we never had the chance to meet her. All I ever heard her family members say was that she was so beautiful that she looked like an angel. I never knew what caused her death. We were told that my mother had her at an incredibly early age. She said her siblings said that my mother was young and very wild. My other two sisters, Cherry and Juanita, and three brothers, Christopher and Billy Joe, were raised in our home. My oldest brother, James, was born after my sister, and Bernice was raised by my mother's oldest sister. My mother had James before she married my father. When my mother met my father, he had an older son, Haskell Jr. I am unsure if he was married to his mother. Sometime after they met, my father and mother were married. My father was the sole provider of our family. He drove a tractor-trailer truck for Hollings Worth and Metromont Material. He was a long-distance driver, so he would leave every Sunday evening and return on Fridays. When he came home late on Friday night, he always brought us Burger King whoppers and fish sandwiches. He always made sure we had the basic things of life. We never went hungry; we always had clothes, shoes, toys for Christmas, and outfits for Easter and the 4th of July. We had all the material basic things of life. My mother was a housewife because my father was very jealous, and he would not allow her to work. Our home was spotless because my mother had a thing about cleanliness. We were raised with morals and respect. My parents drank a lot. On weekends, we would go to one of my father's brother's homes, and all the adults would drink, cuss, fuss, and fight, which was the norm of our weekend family gatherings. On some Saturdays, we would go downtown on Pendleton Street to the local bars with our parents while they drank and partied because they would not leave us alone at home. It was fun because we would be outside in the parking lot behind the bar, playing and eating hot dogs and drinking soft drinks all day while they got drunk. This was one of the highlights of our life because we lived in the country on Fork Shoals Road, and there was nothing to do but play with our cousins when we went to their house with our parents, who went over to drink. I enjoyed going to their homes and the bar on Saturdays. Still, the scary part was when the drinking was over, and we returned home because when they drank, I knew the fighting was coming. My father was very violent toward my mother when they were drinking. My father was an excellent provider but a very mean and cold man. He did not show love or affection, especially toward my mother. I can't recall one time during my childhood that my father ever told any of us that he loved us. I never heard the word love come out of his mouth; I can't remember when my mother even said she loved us. I don't know if it's because I was so traumatized or just so afraid all the time and do not remember. All I remember is that every chance my father got, he would beat my mom so badly. She would be black and blue. Black eyes, busted lips, nose bleeding, just savagely beaten. I remember, as a little girl, five or six years old, being so afraid of my dad because I never knew when he was going to snap and beat my mom. I used to hate it when he came home from work because I knew they were going to drink and he was going to beat Mom. I remember going to bed at night and putting my pillow over my head, pressing it against my ears, and gritting my teeth so I could not hear my mom screaming from being thrown over furniture, falling, and glass breaking from him beating her. I didn't understand why my father was so mean and abusive to my mom, and she was his wife. What made him do this to her when she was his wife? How could he do this to the woman he was supposed to love? I had all these emotions going on inside of me; not knowing how to deal with them is what they even were. I lived each day with so much fear and unhappiness. It became so normal I thought this was how life should be. And so, all this abuse and dysfunction went on from the time I was six to thirteen. On Friday, December 20, 1974, my mother was sick with the flu, and my sister Juanita took her to the doctor, got her some medicine, and brought her home. Mama went to bed, and Juanita cooked so we would have something to eat. My father had come home from work and went out drinking. My youngest brother Billy Joe, who was fourteen at the time, my brother Chris, who was fifteen, and my nephew Lamont, who was my oldest sister Cherry's son, was a baby. He was in bed with my mother. Billy Joe was on a love set in my mother's room watching TV, and my brother Chris was in the living room on the couch sleeping. Billy Joe said that our father came home at about 10:30 that night. He said our father came into the house with his coat on, but that was strange because our father never wore his coat in the house; he always had it across his arm. So, my brother Billy Joe said he thought our father was going back out. He said Daddy came in and leaned on a shift over a fireplace in my parents' bedroom. He said he could tell that Daddy had been drinking. Billy Joe said Daddy told Mama he was hungry and wanted her to get up and fix him something to eat. Billy Joe told Daddy that Mama wasn't feeling well and that Juanita had taken her to the doctor and got her some medicine. He said he told Daddy that Juanita had cooked and that he had to warm the food up. He said Daddy started cussing and said he wasn't warming up a damn thing and that he wanted Mama to get her ass up and warm his food. Billy Joe told Daddy he would warm his food for him. So he got up and started to go warm up Daddy's food, and Daddy said he wasn't going to do shit for him and that Mama's lazy ass was going to do it. Billy Joe said Mama got up out of the bed and started to go to the kitchen. She walked from the side of the bed to the foot of the bed to the kitchen. Where Daddy was standing, Mama's back was to him because a hallway was going into the kitchen. Billy Joe was right in the hallway, and he said just as Mama got right in front of him, Daddy pulled out his gun and shot her in the back, and she fell right at his feet. He said he bent down, and Mama was trying to say something, but blood was coming out of her mouth, and he could not understand what she was trying to say. Billy Joe said Daddy left the gun on the shift he had been leaning against and stood there. The neighbors heard the gunshot and called the police. The neighbor said when she heard the gunshot, she knew my father had killed my mother. She said she and her family used to hear my mother screaming all the time from the beatings. She said she used to tell my mother to leave him because one day he was going to kill her. On Saturday, December 21, 1974, sometime after midnight, my father finally killed my mother; my mother was pronounced dead from a gunshot wound to her back. I was up the street with some friends when one of my friends came and said that my family wanted me to come home because the police were at my house. When I got there, my oldest sister Cherry got home as well. Police and people were everywhere. Everything stopped! The abusive, drinking, fighting, screaming, furniture, and glass being turned over and broken. No more having to put the pillow over my head and press down over my ears and grit my teeth. My mother was dead, and my father was arrested for killing her. At that moment, my whole life went into a whirlwind. The pain was so bad I was dismissed from the real world. That night, we went to my cousin Bucthie's house, where we would go sometimes after Dad had beaten Mama up, and she would leave, but Dad would always talk her into coming back. I never understood that. Mama was buried on Christmas day. They allowed Daddy to attend the funeral. His family was glad, but Mama's family wasn't so happy. I remember him crying and saying he was sorry, but deep inside, I knew his tears and apology were fake. I truly felt that in my heart. After the funeral, Dad went back to jail. My brothers Chris and Bill stayed at home in the same house Mama died in with my oldest sister Cherry, who was around nineteen and had her one-year-old son Lamont. I had lived in hidden fear all my life up to this point because of my dad, and now that he was in jail, I had more fear because my Mama was gone. Life was scary and wild. Bill had to go through so much; he had watched our father kill our mother, and now my dad's sisters were trying to say he was too young to testify against Dad because he didn't know what happened. A story came up somewhere that Dad didn't kill Mama, that she had a crazy boyfriend, and that he shot through the window and killed Mama. Which was a lie. Dad went to trial and was sentenced to 30 years, but he only served five out of the thirty. I never understood that, either. After the trial, our life was tough. There wasn't a lot of family support for us. My cousin Butchie was the only one who looked out for us and helped us. My sister Juanita helped us when she could; she was married and had a family. My brother Chris moved in with my mom's twin brother and his family. Cherry did all she could do, but she was young, and she had her child to raise.

Chapter Two

The beginning of my addiction/parenthood

There were a lot of terrible things that went on during that time. Again, I had mentally checked out. I had already been smoking cigarettes and drinking a little bit. Still, when Daddy killed Mama, my life went even deeper into my pain.

I was thirteen when my dad killed my mother. My world went into a whirlwind. My pain was so bad that I couldn't deal with it. I became so out of control. I just wanted it all to be over. My drinking and smoking went to another level. I started to take drugs. I started taking speed, better known as Black Beauties. In the beginning, they had me so spaced out that I didn't have to deal with my pain, but eventually, I found myself having to take four or five at a time to get numb enough not to feel the pain. This went on for about a year. I was in the streets drinking, smoking, having unprotected sex, sleeping around because I just wanted somebody to love me and make all my pain go away. By the time I turned fourteen, I was introduced to powder cocaine, and my life shifted to a whole new level. My addiction consumed me. I was lost and tripped in it, trying to stay numb so I didn't have to deal with my pain and anger. I was hurting, confused, and mad at everything and everybody. My pain was driving me deeper into destruction. I was getting high every day, all day. I dropped out of school, left home, and just lived anywhere. Wherever I could get high, that's where I would be. I found myself in the company of older men who were drug dealers. Some treated me well because I was young, and so they took advantage of that and fed me all the cocaine I wanted. Others abused me very badly. I was beaten, raped, and passed around to their friends and clients, but I didn't care because they made sure I was high. By the time I turned fifteen, I was strung out on raw cocaine, homeless, and pregnant by a twenty–nine–year–older man who beat me fearlessly. I remember thinking about how I had become the same person I was trying to run away from. My dad and my mom. The only difference was that they drank, and I was drinking and sniffing cocaine. I had my first baby girl, Lisa, and by the grace of God, I didn't get high during my pregnancy, but I was still a mess. And because I had not dealt with my pain as soon as I had her, I was right back in the spiral of my addiction. My daughter was bounced around from one family member to another. During this time, people talked about me, but nobody ever tried to help me understand what was happening to me. At sixteen, I had my second child, Robert, and I didn't get high during my pregnancy with him either, but as soon as he was born, I went right back into it. My daughter Lisa lived mostly between my cousins' and sisters' houses. My son Robert was with me. During this time, I was with a very crazy man who not only beat me but he broke my son's leg when he was five months. When I took him to the emergency room, DSS was called, removed him from my care, and placed him in foster care. This was the beginning of a journey for my children being placed in protective custody because of my drug addiction and not being fit nor having a safe place for them to live. During this time, I had a counselor named Mrs. Nancy Carols, the only person who ever investigated my history. She said she was going to do everything she could to help me. She even said that the system had failed me. Mrs. Nancy helped me get into the Share program, got me started on welfare food stamps, and got me into a low-income appointment. My life was better than before, but I was still being reckless and using drugs. I even lost my apartment because I did not pay my rent, which was only $14.00 a month. My lights were $23.00, and they got cut off. Now, talking about being sick! That was sick. I was back to living with my sister, cousin, and friends. Just whoever would let me stay with them. I was just so tired at this point that I didn't even want to live anymore. I remember during this time sniffing so much raw cocaine that my nose would bleed badly. I had destroyed the tissue in my nose and would continue sniffing. I wanted to die, but little did I know God had His hand on me. He had put Mrs. Nancy in my life, and she would not give up on me. She told me that if I stayed clean and went to AA programs and meetings, she would help me get a job and my place again. At this point, I was exhausted and was willing to do anything. So, I stayed clean, went to AA, and she helped me get another apartment. She also helped me get a job in food service at Greenville General Hospital. I got my daughter back, but my son still had to stay with his foster parents. I worked for a few years and stayed clean for a while. However, the pain was still there, and I again started using drugs, living recklessly, in and out of one relationship after another. By this time, my drug addiction had elevated to crack cocaine, and it was a real beast. It took me to an awful place. I was just tired of everything. I begged God many times to just let me die. I knew about God, but I didn't know Him. Our Aunt Maude took us to church when we were little growing up in the country. We went to Sunday School, but I was never saved. My parents went to church sometimes as well. I even remember that about two weeks before my dad killed my mom, we went to church as a family. Mama said that they were going to stop drinking and start going to church. But that one Sunday was the only time we got to go. I was existing; nothing stopped the emotional pain I was in. No matter how much drugs I did, the pain just got worse and worse. No matter what man I was with, nothing helped. As bad as it was, I did somehow manage to keep a job, mostly to buy drugs. I lost my job at the hospital due to my addiction. Still, I was able to get another job at a janitorial service. I worked for about two years in Greenville, got my son back, got him and my daughter back, and moved to Asheville, North Carolina, with my job in 1982; by the grace of God, even though I was still getting high, I was sniffing cocaine. I moved in with a man and lived with him for about four years until I ran out, moved back to Greenville, and started the same cycle. In 1986, I had my youngest daughter by an older married man. Even though he was married, he was very good to me. But because of my addiction, I used him for his money and mistreated him until he finally just left me alone. I continued with my addiction and reckless living. 1990, I met Dan Fair, who would later become my husband. I met him through my oldest sister, Cherry, and they hung out in some of the same bars. At first, I didn't like him, but he had money, and this was another way for me to continue to use drugs and enjoy my reckless lifestyle. I was so focused on using him for his money that I didn't know that he was the one God would use to answer my cries for help.

Chapter Three

The beginning of my deliverance

Dan was fourteen years older than me. He didn't do drugs, but he did drink. Dan was a very nice man who lived a very stable life. When I met him, he had been working on his job for twenty-five years. He and his mother were also in real estate. He had plenty of money. And that's all that mattered to me. I was still strung out on powdered cocaine, running the streets, and living from pillow to post. Dragging my kids in and out of some horrible places. No matter what I did, he would not give up on me. He used to tell me that he wanted me so badly that it hurt his heart. But I was too mentally sick even to believe that he loved me. Because all I had been shown about love was that it hurt. And so, no matter what he said, I didn't care, and it didn't make me stop using drugs and running the street. At this time, I was living with one of my cousins. I would leave my kids with him and be gone for days. Dan would come by and make sure we had everything we needed. He then started talking to me about getting clean, getting my own house, and getting a job so I could take care of my children. So, I pretended I wanted to get clean to keep him around and continue getting money from him. I told him that I had signed up for a recovery program and that I had to attend classes every day from 10:00 in the morning until 1:00 pm. But, to get there, I had to ride the bus, so he gave me money to ride the bus and get myself something to eat. I took the money he gave me every day, and one of my friend's girls got high. I was lying so much that I had forgotten that I had told Dan that I was going to treatment every day until he asked me if I was still in treatment and when I was going to complete the class. I, with my sick self, boldly said yes, I'm still in treatment, and I'll be graduating on Thursday, May 10, 1991. All he said was ok and drove off. Later that year, he took me and my kids to one of his houses that he owned and said this is your home; stay here and take care of your kids. I felt that somebody cared for me for the first time in a long time. Initially, I didn't have to pay bills or buy food, clothes, anything. He took care of my kids and made us feel safe. He taught me how to drive and bought me a car. He took me to find a job. I started working at Burger King as a cashier and worked my way up to management. Dan showed me how to budget money, write checks, and pay bills. With everything he had done and all the love he showed me, it looked like I would have gotten myself together and done things right. But unfortunately, I didn't. I continue to get high and tell lies. I didn't run the streets as much, but I continued to use drugs; he made sure I worked, paid my bills, and took care of my children. I continued to date Dan, and in 1994, my kids and I moved into Dan's home. At this point, I wasn't using nearly as much. Dan and I had grown closer, and I had begun caring for him. I got another job at Greenville General

Hospital, working in food service. I had started attending the Rock of Ages Baptist Church, where my first cousin, Terry A. King, was the Pastor. I was growing spiritually, but I was still using drugs. I'll never forget; I was at work on a Sunday and heard a voice say, "It is time." I was growing spiritually but hadn't grown much to understand that I was hearing the Voice of God. For seven days, I heard the same voice say, "It Is Time." On that seventh day, I got off work and went home and told Dan to take me to treatment at Charter Rehabilitation Center, and this time, I was serious. Dan took me that evening, and I signed up for my classes. I was able to do outpatients because Dan wasn't using drugs, and I had a safe living environment. My classes were Monday – Friday from 10:00 am until 5:00 pm. On Saturday, I attended NA meetings, got a sponsor, and worked on the 12 Steps of NA. On Sunday, I attended church faithfully. I went to Bible Study, and I attended Sunday School. Now, I understood that the voice I had heard for seven days was the voice of God. I had grown to know Him and accept His love for me, and in 1995, I surrendered my life to Him. Things were going well in my life. Dan, the children, and I were happy. Two months after I surrendered my life, Dan surrendered his life to God, and God began to use us in ministry. On September 29, 1996, Dan asked me to marry him, and I accepted, and on January 4, 1997, we were married. On March 10, 1997, I received my one-year medallion for sobriety. Remember when I talked about the time in 1991 when my friend gave me a certificate for treatment, and when I gave it to Dan, he didn't say anything; he just took the paper and drove off. Well, at my one-year celebration, when it was time for Dan to give some remarks, he pulled out this long yellow folder, and inside it was the fake certificate my friend and I had made. I almost passed out. He said you all know her now, but I knew her when she was sick. I kept this because I loved her so much, and I knew that one day, she would get her life together. Dan also said he kept it so that if I got anything besides myself, he would pull it out and show it to me. That was a perfect and fun day. Dan truly loved me, and he would do anything for me. I came to love him. We continued to work in ministry. We were growing in our faith and praying and seeking God to instruct and guide us in our walk with Him. We began to reach out and evangelize in the community, prison ministry, angel tree, and drug ministry. And on February 21, 1999, I was licensed to preach God's word. That same year, Dan was ordained as a Deacon. Everything was going well; we were enjoying our family, ministry, and working for the kingdom. It was just great. And out of nowhere, my old thinking started showing up. Now, God has delivered me from drugs, and I know I was delivered. I had grown to a place in God through my faith and prayer, and I knew God was faithful and true, and He did not do half jobs. I wasn't craving, nor did I have a desire to use drugs, but the behavior and the lifestyle of my addiction had started creeping back in. In the rooms of NA and AA, they call it "Character Defects." Simple, my flesh had started acting up. There's a saying, "Anything your flesh did have, it will want some more ."I couldn't understand what was happening. But as I look back over my life, I remember crying out to God and asking Him to take my pain and the drugs away, and He did that. And so, I had been so focused on the drugs and the pain that

I didn't even give the behavior and lifestyle I had learned in my addiction any attention. And so, the enemy used it to try and convince me that God had not delivered me. And it worked. I wasn't doing drugs, but I was lying to my husband; I didn't want to have anything to do with him.

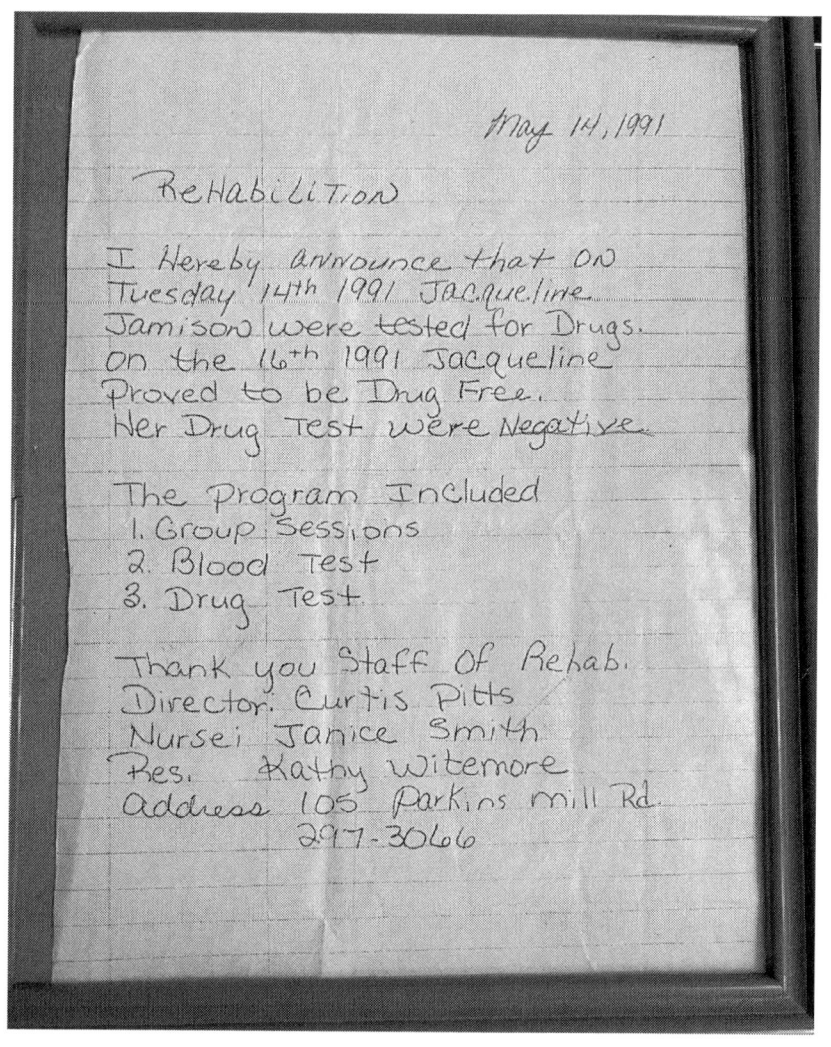

Chapter Four

After My Deliverance

I became very distant and lost focus on the things keeping me. I wasn't praying, studying, or working in ministry as I had been before; I was showing up. Everything that had got me to where I was, I no longer had an interest in. And before I knew it, I found myself in the arms and bed of the devil. The old whoring behavior had shown up. I started dating a man who was smoking crack, drinking every day, and living the reckless lifestyle I used to live. I left my husband, took my children, and moved out of my home into an apartment with my new crackhead boyfriend. I worked at NHC nursing home in Mauldin, South Carolina, as the head cook, making good money. Yes, despite me, God kept his hands on my life. This man drugs me like a caveman. I was buying liquor and crack every day. I hung out in the streets with him, dragging my kids along.

I also had my grandson, my oldest daughter Lisa's son. My husband and I were raising him because I had taught her how to become everything I had been doing; she was a mirror image of me. The only thing I wasn't doing was drugs, but I sure was back deep into my old lifestyle. I was still showing up at the church doing ministry, going to the prisons, and doing outreach with my husband and other church members. I would leave the church, return to my boyfriend, and continue my downward path. By the grace and mercy of God, My Pastor and husband never give up on me.

My husband would only tell me that he knew I had a boyfriend and that I needed to come home. This continued for about four months, and God stripped me of everything. I could no longer pay my bills; I was in so much debt, just running wild. Finally, come to me and go back home. Once again, I cried out to God and asked for his forgiveness. I had once again hurt myself, my family, my Pastor, and my church family and turned my back on God. Once again, they forgave me. God restored me, and I got back on the right path. Through all this, God restored me and elevated me through His anointing. I truly began to understand the love and forgiveness of God. God used All the pain and help I had experienced throughout my life to push me to my purpose. It was all necessary. My pain was not to destroy me but to make me who God had intended for me to be. I was just like Jeremiah when God told him He knew him before he was formed in his mother's womb. I was one of God's chosen vessels. He had picked me to endure everything I went through so that I could testify to who He was and how He uses everything for His purpose. And so I took all my experiences and witnessed others going through the same thing. I embraced all the gifts God had placed in me and helped so many learn to surrender all their hurt and pain to God and allow Him to come into their lives and give them purpose. And so I continued alone with my husband, working in ministry, teaching in prison and drug treatment centers, and telling and sharing my story to lead and guide others to their deliverance and purpose. God had promised me that He would make room for my gifts and bring me before great men. And when I told you, he did exactly that! I was preaching and teaching in places and before people I never imagined. I started attending the Progressive National Baptist Convention with my Pastor and church family, and doors opened for me to teach and preach.

I was asked to teach at the State Convention, the Congress of Christian Education, and other platforms. God even blessed me to go to ITC Theological Seminary in Atlanta, Georgia, where I received a certificate in theological training, N.J. Brockman Learning Center in Greenville, South Carolina, where I received an Associate Degree in Theological Studies, an Honorary Doctrine for Humanity, and God blessed me to teach at the school. And as of today, I'm still teaching. In 2013, I was assisted by one of the senior pastors, Pastor Mae Francis Golden, at Harris Grove Baptist Church in Gray Court, South Carolina, to help her at her church during her illness. I served there until 2014, when God blessed me to be called and elected as the first Female to Pastor Little River Baptist Church in Ware Shoals, South Carolina. I served there until 2018 when I resigned to take care of my husband. He was diagnosed with congestive heart failure. Here again, my life had shifted to another level. Ministry, as I knew it, had become something different.

Chapter Five

Perseverance: WHAT IT TAKES TO CARE FOR A TERMINAL ILL LOVED ONE.

If we are honest, in the African-American culture, it is very rare for family members to care for our loved ones. Now, I do know that there are some, but again not many. And I don't think that, in most cases, it's not that we don't want to; we just don't know how to. Most of the time, we have so much going on in our own lives that we don't see how we can do it.

Looking back over the 31 years (23 married), God blessed me with Dan to spend together; I would never have thought I would become his full-time caretaker in the last five years. Dan was the strength, the mind, and the glue that held our family and everything else together. He was definitely the head of our family. My whole world changed when God blessed me by bringing him into my life.

When I met Dan, I was in a very low and dark place. For 18 years, I had been fighting a terrible crack addiction; I had three children that I had not taken good care of. I went from one place to another, living in houses with no heat, power, water, or food most of the time. My children were in and out of foster homes due to my addictions. I was in so much internal pain due to my father taking my mother's life when I was thirteen.

But in 1989, God blessed me with the presence of Dan. He sent me my lifeline. And when I tell you he was my lifeline, that truly is what he was. God used Dan to restore everything that pain and life had stripped from me. Not only me, but he became a father to my children and my grandchildren. With God's help, he taught me how to love myself so that, in return, I could love my children and, yes, even love him as well.

Now let me say this: we were not saved when God brought Dan into my life. We knew about God, but we did not have a personal relationship with Him. Salvation for both of us came some nine years later after God used Dan to get me together(lol), and that he did. He showed me unconditional love, something I had not ever experienced. And even with all the love he was showing me, I was still sneaking around, lying and getting high. At least, I thought I was. At my first-year celebration with Narcotic Animosity, Dan surprised me with pictures and the fake certificate I gave him stating I had completed a program that I was not even attending. But that's another whole book (LOL).

But he just kept showing unconditional love to my children and me. He owned several houses and allowed my children and me to live in one of his houses. He paid all my bills and made sure that I had food and clothing for my children. He helped me to get a job, manage my finances, open a bank account, write checks, taught me to drive, and bought me a car. I could go on and on about how God used him to help me become the woman I am today. His unconditional love covered me and my family and helped me get serious about my life and my children's lives. And nine years later, I heard the voice of God SAY IT IS TIME! FOR SEVEN DAYS, I HEARD HIM, AND 26 YEARS AGO THAT DAY, I SURRENDERED MY LIFE TO GOD AT ROCK OF AGES BAPTIST CHURCH UNDER THE LEADERSHIP OF PASTOR AND FIRST LADY KING AND I NEVER LOOKED BACK. THAT WAS IN 1995; IN 1996, DAN MADE THE DECISION TO SURRENDER HIS LIFE TO GOD, AND OUR LIFE SHIFTED TO ANOTHER LEVEL. WE WERE MARRIED ON JANUARY 4, 1997, AND WE TRULY WERE A TEAM IN EVERY WAY, FAMILY, MINISTRY JUST THE WHOLE PACKAGE. We became the dream team. Then, in 2005, Dan's health began to fail him; he was diagnosed with congestive heart failure and became limited to what he was used to doing. He could not be the independent and strong one who held everything and everybody together. It was very hard for him because he always wanted to make sure the kids and I were okay. His heart became weaker and weaker over the next 10 years, and then he was diagnosed with kidney disease and high blood pressure. It seemed that every time we went to the doctor, there was something else, but our faith in God kept us sane. Over the years, I watched my husband go from this strong, independent man to a frail and fragile man. Over the next five years, his health deteriorated, and we spent most of the time in hospitals, sometimes nine – ten days at a time. He got so sick that he could no longer drive, walk, or do the essential things to take care of himself. At this time, I realized why God had told me to resign from my assignment of doing ministry as a Pastor. Because now, my ministry was to care for my husband, the one whom God had given me as my first ministry.

And I say all of that to say this: this is how I became a full-time caretaker to my husband!

Again, I promise you that this was not an easy thing to do. But it was the right thing to do. One thing I do know is that as African Americans, we must prepare ourselves to take care of our loved ones because no one else is going to do it like we will.

So, the first thing I had to do was to hear and listen to the voice of God. There was no way I would have resigned from the assignment I knew God had given me, so I stayed at home for three years just caring for my husband. Even knowing God told me, it was very difficult mentally, emotionally, and physically. There were days when I was so depressed because all I did was care for my husband. I barely slept because he needed so much care. I tell you the truth, some days I was very selfish and didn't want to do it; I was mad and angry at God for putting this on me. But I had to hold on to God's strength and power to get through those moments. I had to pick up my cross daily and follow God. I had to deny myself and focus on my husband. I had to remember how he loved me unconditionally and put himself aside many a day to make sure that not only was I ok but that my children were ok.

I had to remember that I was the closest person to him and that he trusted me to help him during this challenging time. I know it had to be heartbreaking for him when he was so used to taking care of our family. His pride was hurt, and he felt ashamed. So, I not only had to face my concerns and fears, but I also had to face his as well. I had to make sure that he knew, no matter what, that I was not going to abandon him, nor was I going to put him in a nursing home. With the strength and wisdom of God, I had to provide stability and spiritual hope and assure him that he was loved and valued and that his life was valued. I had to always put his emotional needs before mine. Everything about me was secondary. I had to encourage him even when I was discouraged. I had to tell him to trust God and hold on to his faith in God and to keep fighting even when, on most days, I did not have faith in God and wanted so badly to give up. There were days when I looked at Dan and had to fight back my tears and fears so that he could go on. Nothing during this time was about me but totally about him. Even on the days when he would become so angry and mean and say things to me that were hurtful because of his frustration, I still had to find the strength to encourage him when he felt as if God was punishing him, even though at times, I felt the same way. As his caretaker, I didn't have the time for my feelings to be hurt because I had to put aside my own emotions and put his needs first.

I had to make many sacrifices during this time and put my needs aside. I could no longer have and be a part of a social circle; I didn't have any activities I could attend because he required all of my attention. I was operating on very little sleep most days, if any. I had become totally numb; I didn't feel anything. As my husband's full-time caretaker, my emotions fluctuated wildly across many emotions. It's sad and hard to say and even face sometimes, but there were times when I begged God to let it end; I prayed that God would let Dan die for his suffering would end, but then I would feel guilty. I would even hate myself for even feeling this way. I felt helpless, anxious, stressed, depressed, and angry all at once.

During all these mixed emotions, I couldn't work out and walk as I was used to, so food became my way of escape. And everything I had worked so hard for was gone. I gained all the weight back that I had lost and then some. This really sent my emotions into a whirlwind. At times, I felt like I had no source of support for myself or no outlet available. I felt so isolated from my family and friends, but I knew I had to take care of my husband. For months, I watched my husband slowly dying, and there was nothing I could do to stop it. All I could do was make sure he was clean, comfortable, and loved. Once he stopped eating and drinking, it really became emotionally and mentally draining.

For three and a half years, my days consisted of taking care of my husband. It was as if I no longer existed; all my focus was on Dan. My days started at 4:30 every morning unless the night was so rough that I didn't get any rest. I would get up, wake my grandson Pebo up for work, and then take a few minutes for God and me. I would pray, take my meds, eat a bowl of cereal, drink a cup of coffee, take a bath, and get dressed; by then, it was about 5:30. I would prepare Dan's meds to get his cardiomems pilliard ready, so I could put him on it to register his fluid intake; this consisted of lifting the upper part of his body and pulling him onto the pilliard for the pilliar to register. The next step was to stick his finger to check his sugar and then his oxygen. Once that was completed, it was time to undress him for his bath. Even though he was bedridden and didn't have much movement, I gave him a full bath every day, plus I would oil down his skin to prevent bed sores. And let me add, in three years, Dan didn't have not one bed sore. I cut his hair, shaved him once a week, and cut his toenails. I changed his bed linning as often as I needed to, which took rolling him over from one side of the bed, removing the dirty lining, and replacing it with clean lining. Until the last year of his life, I dressed him daily in clean pajamas and put powder and lotion on him so he would smell good. This made him feel better. Then, once he lost all mobility and movement, I could no longer put his bottom pajamas on because he had to put bed pads underneath him for when he used the restroom; it was easier to just clean him. In his condition, it hurt him to his heart not to be able to care for himself, and he was too ashamed to have a stranger come in and take care of him, so as his wife, his soulmate, it was my responsibility to care for him. There was no way I would have allowed him to feel ashamed of being sick and have someone he didn't know to care for him. Then, I would prepare his breakfast, and by then, he would be totally exhausted from all that and sleep for a few hours until I woke him up for noonday meds, lunch, and to change him and the bed. I would repeat this all throughout the day until evening around 6:00 to give him his dinner and night meds. By this time of day, I would be exhausted, but I did my best not to let him see it. But sometimes he did, and he would say my baby needs a vacation; I see it in your eyes; you are exhausted, but I would try to reassure him that I was ok.

There were many who told me I needed to look into putting Dan in a nursing home. I would think about it, but I just could not bring myself to do it. I knew what it took to take care of him, and I knew how he could be mean and hard to deal with at times. I knew how he made me want to walk away, so I knew nobody would take care of him the way I did. It was totally my dependence on God and God's strength; otherwise, there was no way I could have done all that I had to do nor endure all I did if it had not been for the lord. If I don't know anything else, I know I know the lord, and he knows and cares for me.

I will tell anybody, if you have a loved one who is terminally ill, please pray and seek God for direction and strength to take care of them. Just don't throw them in a nursing home. Nobody is going to take care of them like you!!! I never thought I would have to do it, but as I look back now, I'm thankful that God chose me to take care of my husband. I learned so much about him and myself, and I truly got to know God in a more intimate way. I can be a doctor and a nurse; all I really need are the papers because I have hands-on experience.

On July 27, 2020, Dan died. I had never felt this kind of pain. My whole life changed; everything was different, and I didn't know what to do. Dan and I had shared 30 years together, and now it was just me. The first few months were rough. I was so used to him being with me, and now it was just me. I would go through the day still focusing on taking care of him. I didn't sleep, couldn't sleep. Everything in my home reminded me of him. I cried so much until I had no more tears. I would lie on the bed, look at his pictures on my phone, and wrap myself up in one of his sweat jackets so I could smell him for hours until I dozed off. Then I would wake up looking for him, and the realness of his death would hit me again. My family tried to be there for me, but it didn't help. The pain was crippling; I missed Dan so much. I felt myself slipping into a very dark place. I couldn't even pray. And to be honest, even though when things had gotten so bad that I had asked God to take Dan, now that he had, I was very angry!!

Made in the USA
Columbia, SC
14 June 2024

36584972R00020